Traffic Jams: Analysing Everyday Life through
the Immanent Materialism of Deleuze & Guattari

Traffic Jams

Analysing Everyday Life through the Immanent Materialism of Deleuze & Guattari

David R. Cole

dead letter office

BABEL Working Group

punctum books ✶ brooklyn, ny

 Traffic Jams: Analysing Everyday Life Through the
Immanent Materialism of Deleuze & Guattari
© David R Cole, 2013.

http://creativecommons.org/licenses/by-nc-nd/3.0/

This work is Open Access, which means that you are free to copy, distribute, display, and perform the work as long as you clearly attribute the work to the authors, that you do not use this work for commercial gain in any form whatsoever, and that you in no way alter, transform, or build upon the work outside of its normal use in academic scholarship without express permission of the author and the publisher of this volume. For any reuse or distribution, you must make clear to others the license terms of this work.

First published in 2013 by
dead letter office, BABEL Working Group
an imprint of punctum books
Brooklyn, New York

The **BABEL Working Group** is a collective and desiring-assemblage of scholar-gypsies with no leaders or followers, no top and no bottom, and only a middle. BABEL roams and stalks the ruins of the post-historical university as a multiplicity, a pack, looking for other roaming packs and multiplicities with which to cohabit and build temporary shelters for intellectual vagabonds. We also take in strays.

ISBN-10: 0615767001
ISBN-13: 978-0615767000

All images on cover and inside of book are still-captures from Jean-Luc Godard's film *Weekend* (1967).

Abstract

This dead letter presents an exploration of the immanent materialism of Deleuze & Guattari as theorised in *A Thousand Plateaus* as a means to analysing everyday life. The evidence consists of art, film and objects from life that relate to and suggest the complex ways in which we are affected by traffic jams. Reciprocating substrata of everyday life build upon the unconscious, and show how the abstract turbulence of everyday life forms eddies and flows that may be followed and (re)presented. The immanent materialism of Deleuze & Guattari is a philosophical construction that leads to the formation of 'plateaus' as they were executed in *A Thousand Plateaus*. The plateau of this dead letter is *[21 October 2011: The Petro-Citizen]* and is populated with traffic jams, car crashes, global environmental concerns and the psychological and sociological contingencies that accompany the petro-citizen. Connections between the strata that make up the plateau of the petro-citizen will deliberately be left as open-ended and speculative to show how the petro-citizen functions as a flagrant construct in everyday life, which includes the desire for petrol and explains the resulting panpsychic petro-political landscape. The double-articulation of the plateau depends upon the ways in which the petro-citizen and petro-politics create reciprocating realms of motivation and drive that tend towards contemporary double-articulation, paradox and contradiction with respect to the usages of oil. This double-articulation results in a multiple chequered flag or illusionary global end-game that designates the current human relationships with oil.

Table of Contents

Introduction	1
The Petro-Citizen	5
Immanent Materialisms of Everyday Life	9
Car Crashes and the Death Drive	15
Time-images of Car Crashes and Traffic Jams	19
Libidinal Carism	23
The Plateau of the Petro-Citizen	27
Global Car Crashes and Traffic Jams / China & the North Pacific Gyre	33
Epilogue—Ode to Michael Douglas	39
References	41

Traffic Jams

Analysing Everyday Life through the Immanent Materialism of Deleuze & Guattari

David R. Cole

§ INTRODUCTION

What is everyday life? The singularity within this question, and by degrees, this paper, is formed by the conjunction of often simultaneous, subjective, narrative structures that allow one to explain everyday life in terms of events and occurrences in sequence, and also the particular, objective historical context that one finds oneself embroiled within; this aspect of everyday life is foregrounded by and through political economics. The idea of everyday life in this paper is henceforth diverted from the structural critique or objective sociology that Henri Lefebvre (2002) enacted, and aligned with the practice of everyday life as described by Michel de Certeau (1988). Certeau famously stated that in order to become embroiled within the practices of everyday life, one should walk around urban areas, and this strategy has resonance here, because such a tactic predominantly relieves one of car travel. Certeau's practice of thinking about embedded narratives through walking enables the tactics and strategies of everyday life to come to the fore, and these ideas join well with Deleuze and Guattari's affective politics as represented in *A Thousand Plateaus* (1998). Everyday life in this paper is a form of reflexive, affective politics. This politics includes: art, non-organic life, and thinking through the elements of contemporary existence until one begins to discern the plateau of everyday life as a concurrent, reciprocating reality, and a potential maelstrom of non-human becomings. I have termed this engrained and fluvial reality as the 'petro-citizen,' both as a critical marker of contemporary existence and as a portal for understanding the political manipulation of the present.

§ THE PETRO-CITIZEN

We are petro-citizens. This statement is true even if we reject the everyday use of cars, if we only use public transport, or if we believe in a green solution to impending environmental catastrophe. The petro-citizen is not a negative assessment with respect to everyday life; but it is a fitting term, that sums up many of the most vital elements of becoming involved with everyday life. Populations have been turned into packs of consumers through the economic and governmental processes of the last twenty-five years (Kelly 1999), and everything that we consume depends in some way on petrol. Parallel to this dependence, the thought of traffic jams sits inside of us, and creates emotional responses to events, some of which we may be barely aware. These responses and sentiments to everyday life are aligned through Deleuze & Guattari's rhizomatics (1988) with pipelines of global capital that have increased the accessibility and proliferation of petrol with subjectivity. The wealth that is being created due to petrol consumption is reinvested in everyday life as complementary and alternative forms of economic activity. The economy is therefore driven and accelerated by petrol and the many other products of oil that we use, for example, plastics. George Bush said that we are "addicted to oil." This is an underestimation of the connection between subjectivity and oil. The micro-dynamics of traffic combined with the macro politics of oil is more than an addiction. This "more than" may be understood through the ways in which the reality of traffic jams transmutes into different behaviours and planes that intersect with and manifest in everyday life. For example, for many commuters, the drive to and from work intersects with feelings of powerlessness, frustration, and an inability to change circumstances; which is also conjunctive with road expansion, car production, satellite towns, and the car parks of shopping malls. The petro-citizen dutifully consumes petrol via buying their food at the supermarket, the citizens ingest the smell of the fumes that lingers in the air, and their bodies become impregnated with oily substances . . . .

The designation of the petro-citizen allows us to talk about everyday life in a new way. Such is life, as we are now thoroughly riven by oil.

This means that our minds are in many ways dictated to by oily power concerns, which have been termed as petro-politics (see Negarestani 2008). The process that this politics determines may be understood as the hollowing out of subjectivity by oil, and the replacement of the self with the actions necessary to keep the economic flows of petrol consumption working. In order to achieve this, one's actions are packaged and represented as the oscillation between work-leisure and the consumptive attitudes that are involved with the petro-politics of the work-leisure range. For example, television programmes such as the U.K.'s *Top Gear* work in this range by rhetorically closing down options that are other than the petro-plateau; and by making the existence of alterative realities to oil seem absurd and irrelevant. Car advertising does a similar job, aligning sex, freedom, self-worth and vitality to the petro domain. The petro-citizen absorbs all these influences as everyday life.

The difference that this letter wishes to communicate can be demonstrated through the opening scene to Jean-Luc Goddard's *Weekend*. The camera pans along the traffic jam, and records the absurdity and heartbreak of the situation. The traffic jam stretches on inexorably and strangely, and is an enmeshed chain of events. This cinematographic moment allows one to gain insight into the penetrating reality of traffic jams. This film raises consciousness of the ways in which the multiple aspects of traffic jams sit inside of us, and determine emotional and rational responses to phenomena long after one has driven clear of the hold up. To understand this connectivity further, one must delve into the immanent materialism that underpins this piece.

§ IMMANENT MATERIALISMS OF EVERYDAY LIFE

A Thousand Plateaus (1988) is an integrated philosophical system. One might say that the plateaus have no start and no end, though one is able to reconstruct their evolution through understanding the influences and intentions of the authors. Deleuze borrows terms and concepts from the history of philosophy. Guattari worked through psychoanalytic and political conceptions of the Real. The first point about the plateaus is that they mean to say something important about the unconscious. Deleuze and Guattari worked out a means to link economics with the unconscious in their first joint book, *Anti-Oedipus* (1984). This was essentially achieved by closely meshing Freud with Marx, and by taking the most non-normative approach possible to this alignment. *Anti-Oedipus* is a breakthrough text in terms of understanding how the unconscious works on a social and economic plane, and because it unties the stranglehold of Oedipus on the unconscious. *A Thousand Plateaus* goes further than *Anti-Oedipus* in that the unconscious is set free from the universal, historically dialectical time of Marx and given specific dates and foci. The focus of this writing is [traffic jams—2011]; and this determines a plateau that continually interacts with the unconscious and everyday life.

Immanent materialism is here an example of a new materialism (Coole and Frost 2010). This means that the ways in which one understands materialism is in a state of constant re-evaluation. Thoughts, the imagination, and the unconscious are included in this immanent materialist analysis, as the restructuring of materialist flows is in a state of perpetual flux. One could cogently ask about the nature of the real, given the mixture of thoughts and actual life that immanent materialism somewhat perilously demarcates (see Brassier 2011). Deleuze (1995) answered this question in terms of the careful synthesis and analysis of everyday life. One isn't interested in everything to do with everyday life, but in the intersections and dynamics of everyday life that emerge in the gaps between the packages of thought and the flows of material objects that one can follow. There is a form of chaos theory at work here, yet this theory is mitigated by and blended with philosophy. The precise material model of everyday life that one derives according to immanent materialism must say something about agency and politics. Everyday life flows through us, yet it is also out there in the world as a combinational matrix that subjugates and divides. Everyday life started long before we were born and will continue after we are dead, yet "everyday life" also has a particular reality that we may describe today in terms of the Real. This letter does work in this arena by locating traffic jams and the petro-citizen as a contemporary plateau for 2011 and putting them into conceptual and theoretical action.

The immanent materialism of this writing responds to a vitalist concept of time. This means that the dynamic interactions of everyday life that are formed in the unconscious are extended through time as a vital energy in "things" (see Bennett 2010). One could say that the ways in which traffic jams affect us determines a form of duration or *durée*, which is an accumulating mode of understanding time. The accumulating mode of time adds to the sense of time as repetition, absurdity, boredom and sameness. Not only does the powerlessness of traffic jams capture one's unconscious, it also stretches and plays with time. The endless repetition of the experience of traffic jams in one's life requires a strict vitalism, which animates the ways in which the contemplation and representation of traffic jams may alter reality. This alteration links the immanent materialism of this letter to art, and shows how traffic jams can be taken out of context and given new and different life. This connection to artwork also corresponds to the Spinozism (see, for example, Gatens 1996) that is functioning here, in that representations of traffic jams uncover affect in both the viewer and doer of the art. For example, in Goddard's film, *Weekend*, the positioning of the narration and viewing is deliberately complicated to increase the impact of the traffic jams and car crashes. The affect of traffic jams is a dynamic collision of forces that can set off random and unforeseen events, as well as perpetual "stuckness." Traffic jams can be dramatic, moving, unearthly, and awe-inspiring. In this sense, the traffic jam determines a mode of social production without ownership that one may take from Marx, and a plane of immanence that attempts to establish differences in kind. These differences in kind are importantly distinguished from Kantian differences, in that the difference that immanent materialism establishes is not involved with transcendence or the subject "I" (Kant 1933). Phenomenology is circumvented through immanent materialism by setting the subject free of its perceptual bindings. The main strategy that Deleuze & Guattari (1988) use to free one of perceptual binding is the insertion of the multiple into argumentation. For example, the traffic jam could be seen as one homogeneous nightmare, or taken apart through close inspection of its component parts. However, at the heart of this unbinding action, and in order to cope with the dictates of the Real in an expanded and convoluted subject, lies an inevitable confrontation with death. In between the spaces of the traffic jam, both in our minds and in reality — are car crashes. The insertion of car crashes into the immanent materialism of traffic jams brings us closer to the reality of everyday life.

§ Car Crashes and the Death Drive

The construction of a plane of immanence with respect to the everyday life of traffic jams includes the reality of car crashes. The unconscious is activated at this point, as the chaos of non-determinate affect involved with a car crash seeps into consciousness. This thought production could manifest as a sudden panic attack whilst driving, or as a certain atmosphere of fear that one might discern as one enters a roundabout or in a car park. Andy Warhol's *Pink Car Crash* (1963), one of a sequence of paintings in a "disaster" series, demonstrates the affect of fear as a suburban family clamber out of their upturned car. One can see a white picket fence behind the car crash, which adds to the affect in that the death drive has arrived in familiar suburbia. Everyday life is therefore connected to the death drive, and everyday life is also made other through this piece of art. *Pink Car Crash* has a visceral affect on the viewer in that the ways in which one may perceive are engaged and reversed. That could be you struggling to get out of your car after your next trip to the shops. After viewing this picture that thought could lodge itself in your mind every time that you get into your car. The death drive wells up in the mind through car crashes, and this drive is a crucial aspect in the construction of what we might call the traffic unconscious (see Deleuze 1997). The point here is not that immanent materialism consists only of focusing on death, or by revelling in the negative possibilities associated with car travel, but that the immanence of car crashes, as *Pink Car* demonstrates, communicates an overwhelming and absolute reality.

The everyday reality of car crashes is full of material that one may add to the traffic jam plane of immanence. The artists Ben Quilty and Tom McGrath have painted the wrecks of cars after head-on collisions. The wreckage of the car is abstracted from context — one doesn't see anyone struggling to get out of the wreck, or where the car has been crashed. The car wreck is therefore a singular object, full of its own life, and not possessing a clear back narrative or framing story. The point here is that the unconscious, consumed by the death drive, doesn't necessarily free-associate through the contemplation of images to fill in every possibility about their existence. Rather, the objects may take on their own lives, the car wrecks are allowed to "become other" through immanent materialism. The application of *A Thousand Plateaus* to everyday life concentrates and focuses on the production of the new (see Deleuze and Guattari 1988), and gives rise to different realities that define material flows of objects and ideas. In the case of the images of car wrecks, these flows are an amalgam of twisted metal, halted desires, indentation, contortion, ruptures, and wounds. The affects that are extracted from the images of car wrecks include the becoming-dislocated of the car crash. The car crash is henceforth bestowed with agency that moves between notions of speed, progress, and death. The car crash defines a path to the wreckers' yard; it is the place that we are heading to whenever we turn on the transmission. Death haunts the roads, it moves through our vehicles; death takes hold of the steering wheel . . . .

§ TIME-IMAGES OF CAR CRASHES AND TRAFFIC JAMS

The car crash is a moment in time as represented by paintings of car wrecks; the car crash is also a sequence of moments that has led to the final wreckage. This sequencing can be seen in Andy Warhol's *Green Burning Car* (1963). *The Green Burning Car* (1963) is a series of slides that presents an upturned burning car in a front yard with a large tree and house. However, Warhol plays with our perception of the car crash by repeating and treating the same image. The car burns in different places on the slide, and is accompanied by the same two figures, one walking away from the burning car, the other pinned to a tree. One gains the perception that there is action and sequence embedded in these images by the layout; but the truth is that Warhol has represented stasis and the immobility of a crash through one burning car. In Deleuzian terms, *Green Burning*

Car is an example of a lapsed time-image, wherein movement and time are conjoined in an imagistic framework:

> There is thus no longer association through metaphor or metonymy, but relinkage on the literal image; there is no longer linkage of associated images, but only relinkages of independent images. Instead of one after the other, there is one image *plus* another; and each shot is deframed in relation to the framing of the following shot." (Deleuze 1989, 205)

In Dena Schuckit's *Zagged* (2010), the time-image is a collage of an inverted, crippled, traffic jam and a rupture point, where an explosion of colour and form represents the suture of a car crash. The painting comes out of the frame and impresses the reality of the car crash on the viewer. This dynamic framing is a time-image in that the picture is a representation of various shots taken from the perspective of someone watching a car crash. Firstly, the traffic moves along in a traffic jam, a car crash takes place — there is an explosion involved with the crash — and pieces of wreckage and flesh fly out of the scene. All of the other cars in the traffic jam are now implicated in the crash, and crash themselves through inversion. This image is not a metaphor or metonymy for everyday life, but a lapsed time-image that shows how the pieces of a car crash fit together and relate to one another. According to immanent materialism, one does not interpret the picture and imbue it with alternative meanings; rather, one allows the interrelated material flows to be brought forth and into life through immanence. This process and methodology stems in part from the artistic movements of Surrealism, Dada, the Situationists, and constructivism. One can transform everyday objects and create new realities according to the principles of incongruity and surprise. The creative unconscious is employed in terms of creating "ready-made" artefacts that disrupt normative assumptions with respect to function and form. Hence, a car crash could be known as a "Broken Mechanical Flower," due to the patterns of glass, plastic and metal, a traffic jam is an instance of "car sickness." Science fiction movies often blow up cars and include traffic jams as special effects, and this is particularly effective strategy for disrupting the sense of normality that one might associate with the image(s). The lapsed time-image is therefore a flexible and inverting schema for understanding the ways in which car crashes and traffic jams represent reality, and impinge upon everyday life and the unconscious.

§ Libidinal Carism

The everyday life of petro-politics implies a certain relationship with libidinal forces, which could be expressed through the phrase, "libidinal carism." People begin to worship their cars. This relationship is loving, fetishized, sexual and intimate. The becoming involved here importantly signifies a certain process of car-modification. One can fit enormous speakers to the back of the vehicle, use the back end of the car for pole dancing, or turn one's van into a science fiction transportation device. The focus here is not to dismiss these consequences of "libidinal carism" as other than the "normal" relationship that one might want to develop between oneself and one's car, but to understand that these behaviours may be studied and incorporated into the notion of everyday life that this letter is articulating with reference to immanent materialism. In this case, the rubric is that of ethology, or the study of social organization from a biological perspective (see Gatens 1996). The whole panoply of petro-politics comes into view at this point, as the libidinal forces involved with "carism" carry with them immense social tendencies and the ways in which life is currently organised. For example, the connection between car advertising, town planning, and roads creates a landscape through which one is able to study current behaviours and forms of the pack. One is 'turned on' through car advertisement, usually with reference to sex, status, or freedom. This energy is henceforth packaged and managed through one's use of the car in the town where one lives — for example, in the drive to work, going to school, or in the pursuit of leisure. Finally, this criss-crossing map and trace of one's life may be seen from above in the density of the traffic and in the exact form of the roads upon which one travels everyday. The ethology of everyday life is therefore represented through the relationship between car advertising and roads, as well as the becomings and machinery involved with human-car modification.

The fictional novel that has come closest to an immanent materialism of everyday life and the petro-citizen is J.G. Ballard's *Crash* (1973). David Cronenberg made Ballard's hallucinogenic tale into a film (1996) — and the book and the film demonstrate many of the principles of libidinal carism. Ballard wrote:

> I looked through the colour photographs in the magazines; in all of them the motor-car in one style or another figured as the centrepiece — pleasant images of young couples in group intercourse around an American convertible parked in a placid meadow; a middle-aged businessman naked with his secretary in the rear seat of his Mercedes; homosexuals undressing each other at a roadside picnic; teenagers in an orgy of motorised sex on a two-tier vehicle transporter, moving in and out of lashed-down cars; and throughout these pages the gleam of instrument panels and window louvres, the sheen on over-polished vinyl reflecting the soft belly of a stomach or a thigh, the forests of pubic hair that grew from every corner of these motor-car compartments. (Ballard 1973, 104)

Cars and humans are thoroughly entwined in this novel and film. Unfortunately, Cronenberg took the ideas in the book literally and represented the conflagration of humans and machines in a straightforward manner. The deployment of immanent materialism requires innovation and a more creatively innovative extension from the literal representation of ideas. The analysis of everyday life is well served by the novel as the libidinal intent is presented without emotion and in a non-interpretive manner, as one can see from the passage from the novel *Crash* above. In Deleuze & Guattari's (1984; 1988) terms, Cronenberg has ignored the tenets of the body without organs (BwO), and the practises necessary to create a work of art that successfully deals with desire in a non-representational fashion. The film version of *Crash* presents a highly stylised version of "libidinal carism" without the satire and irony required to make the ideas gel. Rather, the film wallows in pornography, and does not allow the material flows of sexualised action to circulate; the car crash therefore represents an analogy with orgasm in the film and not multi-dimensional lapsed time-images (see Deleuze 1989, 45) that additively combine cars, sex, desire, and death.

The film of *Crash* presents a moment of impact that is a direct transference from the flesh and sexuality of the body into the machine functioning of the car. This transference is compounded by the filmic choices made in the production of the film. In contrast, the book present multiple moments of impact, where flesh and machine communicate through sexuality in a multiple and complex manner. As such, libidinal carism transmutes and crosses over into everyday life, and may be understood as an important principle of the petro-citizen.

§ THE PLATEAU OF THE PETRO-CITIZEN

The exact political positioning of the petro-citizen is a convoluted and reflexive construction. This is in line with the politics of immanent materialism, which takes relevant political movements, and follows the material flows that these movements present — in this case, to aid with the analysis of everyday life and the petro-citizen. For example, the global liberal market economics of the present situation flows through the petro-citizen, as the connections to capital, cars, petrol consumption, and the products of oil is immanent to everyday life. With this in mind, "oil is an ineluctable mirage and brake on any form of lasting political innovation" (Toscano 2010, 2). The petro-politics of everyday life sits behind the instances that one may present to sustain the thesis of the petro-citizen as a shadow, or as an oily smudge on the clarity of the concepts involved. This is especially pertinent with respect to the political analysis of the situation. The immense wealth that oil produces encourages lies, deception, and the artificial positioning of power elites who are interested in the capital flows of oil, yet also pretending to side with green solutions to environmental problems. Most politicians still vote for road construction, the investment and jobs of car factories, and the diplomatic appeasement of oil producing nations. The result in terms of politics is a shady plateau, which we have termed as the petro-citizen, and this is an expanded version of subjectivity that fully embraces the conglomerations of oil in everyday life. Individuals or groups may choose to ethically oppose many of the consequences of the global domination of oil. However, such opposition is not enough to stem the tide of the invasion of the plateau by the petro-citizen and petro-politics. The machinery of capitalism and oil within which we now live, encourages domestication, trauma and subjugation to capital flows that are connected to oil production. These processes of invasion by the petro-citizen and petro-politics have a plethora of diverse strategies at hand, which cannot be straightforwardly calculated or quantified, but define an indeterminate mutational thesis and rolling plane of immanence:

> This immense multiplicity of factors is in complete opposition to the harshness of

determinism, into which, by breaking [determinism] down into endless action and reaction, it [immanent materialism] introduces cleavage and discord at every turn. (Focillon 1992, 156)

This is why one needs to accept the tenets of immanent materialism to understand how the petro-citizen and petro-politics function. Immanent materialism has an aleatory structure, which one may understand with reference to concepts such as the machinic phylum. The machinic phylum demonstrates how the organic and inorganic create series and permutations according to immanent materialism, and in the case of this letter, these series populate everyday life and the petro-citizen. The petro-citizen is subject to evolution, yet this evolution is accelerated and mutated through the petro-political influences of oil. The organic and the inorganic work together in the formation of petro-citizens, and this formation is a chequered flag in terms of drawing one forward to understand and participate in everyday life. The chequered flag is not an artificial end-point to our understanding of plateau of the petro-citizen, but adds to libidinal motivation. The chequered flag signals an accelerating element in everyday life.

The concept of libidinal carism moves one in time, on the plateau of the petro-citizen, and towards the chequered flag; yet this time is itself constructed as a vital time-image, and is therefore subject to the analysis of everyday life that we are performing. The analysis of the everyday is therefore always a double movement. One understands more about everyday life through the application of immanent materialism to the plateau of the petro-citizen; however, there are always elements within the analysis that sit across from and through the plane of immanence, and therefore escape immediate attention. One therefore enters into a form of reciprocal ontogenesis with respect to constructing the plane of the petro-citizen, and in gaining knowledge about everyday life. This is a process of individuation as described by Simondon:

> Individuation does not only produce the individual. One ought not skip quickly over the step of individuation in order to arrive at that last reality that is the individual. One ought to try to know the ontogenesis in the entire development of that reality and get to know the individual in terms of individuation rather than individuation in terms of the individual. (Simondon 1964, 4)

The individual or group that one may understand as the petro-citizen includes an intense process of individuation or ontogenesis. This is a double-layered chequered flag that is drawing our civilization forward, below, and through the plateau of the petro-citizen and petro-politics. This level of connection includes decay, vitalism, virality, speed, accelerationism, and peak oil. If we are heading towards a tipping point in terms of the global economy and oil, it will be registered in this subaltern level or the second chequered flag of the plateau of petro-citizen. Deleuze described the relationship between the two levels of the plateau of the petro-citizen in *The Logic of Sense* (1990), where he examined the nature of the series in literature and how these series relate to aleatory and singular factors. Reality is formed through the reciprocity between series, because, "[r]eality is not only actual series, but rather relations of reciprocal determinations between actual and ideal series through a medium they share, the surface of changing intensities" (Williams 2009, 103). Deleuze derived this psychoanalytic interpretation of reality from his reading of Lacan through Melanie Klein, and he shows how one comes to understand reality through the oscillations between different levels or strata.

In *The Logic of Sense*, Deleuze used *Alice in Wonderland* to explain this oscillation, and in our analysis of everyday life, one may apply this notion to the plateau of the petro-citizen. Alice changes in form as she travels through the labyrinth of her mind (and life). The petro-citizen changes in form as one constructs the plane whereby the petro-citizen may exist — including the subjectivating elements that one can draw from contemporary narrative, economics and life. The construction of the petro-citizen should not be an entrapment on the plane of oily influence, but will help to understand the ways in which, for example, art can represent reality. There is therefore a necessary oscillation between the different planes in the plateau of the petro-citizen. The chequered flags that draw us forward to understand the petro-citizen also can knock us backwards, and drop us into a pit of gooey, dark substance. We can just as easily end up stranded on the motorway, clogged and blocked with cars, as we can find our way through the congestion, and construct a workable petro-citizen existence. Immanent materialism keeps the two options open and simultaneous; we don't have to take either road, as the two levels of the petro-citizen plateau are working together to construct multiple realities in everyday life . . . .

§ GLOBAL CAR CRASHES AND TRAFFIC JAMS / CHINA & THE NORTH PACIFIC GYRE

The plateau of the petro-citizen forms individuals and herds that consume and exist within the context of petro-politics, and this formation now extends around the globe (see Toscano 2010). One of the clearest consequences of this spread of the petro-citizen is the consumptive practices and growth of cars in China. The longest traffic jams in the world are now in Beijing. There are chthonic relationships between the ways in which the individuation of petro-politics forms citizens and the consumptive patterning and global consequences of these drives; and these should also be explored. One might say that the traffic jams in China represent a mode of organization that infiltrates the ways in which one might now conceive of freedom. The drives that one exhibits in order to consume and exist within the context of petro-politics correspond to relationships that the drives inscribe around the globe. The point isn't that the citizens of China want to merely copy the lifestyle choices of the West. The point is that petro-politics influences the choices of the Chinese as an unremitting drive that pushes them along to overtake the West. The consequences in terms of resource depletion and potential environmental disaster are clear. The internal conflicts that the choices of the emerging Chinese petro-citizens will produce and are producing are more convoluted. This is because the economies of the West and China are now integrated in one global capitalist system, so that the increases in wealth in China are intimately connected to the fortunes (and even misfortunes) of the West through global market economics. One could say that the traffic jams in China burrow through and emerge around the globe as stops and starts in apparently unrelated economic activity. One feels this connection in terms of freedom:

> Oh, the poor bird that felt free and now strikes the walls of this cage! Woe, when you feel homesick for the land as if it had offered more freedom – and there is no longer any land. (Nietzsche 2001, 181)

Nietzsche expressed the workings of immanent materialism in terms of subjectivity and freedom. Currently, the internet may be used to communicate the ideas of immanent materialism simultaneously and concurrently around the globe. Chinese citizens can do research on American and European lifestyles and replicate these habits in their own terrain. This means that, for example, the notion of violent revolution and the overthrow of oppressive regimes can now happen through a combination of various electronically mediated and organised social media and acts of rebellion, which could ultimately threaten the continued predominance of the Chinese communist party: "[w]ithin this MySpace version of the electronic agora, cybernetic communism is mainstream and unexceptional. What had once been a revolutionary dream is now an enjoyable part of everyday life" (Barbrook 2007, 12). The introduction of the internet into the equations of the petro-citizen enables contradictory and unforeseen consequences in its construction. For example, a photograph of a traffic jam in Sao Paulo may be connected on the internet to an exhibition of suspended cars in Oslo, paintings of stylised car deaths in crashes in Los Angeles, and also to a representation of "libidinal carism" in Kiev. The plethora of meanings that one can extract from such multiple connectivities and the confluence of imagery gives rise to the creativity and artistic possibilities of immanent materialism. This is an affective movement, demonstrating mobile innovations and a highly developed sense of conceptual construction. One is never able to fully relax, and think that immanent materialism has been completely realised, as immanent materialism does not represent a closed or ideal system. Rather, the forces and drives must be ceaselessly explored and developed in new works of (re)creation....

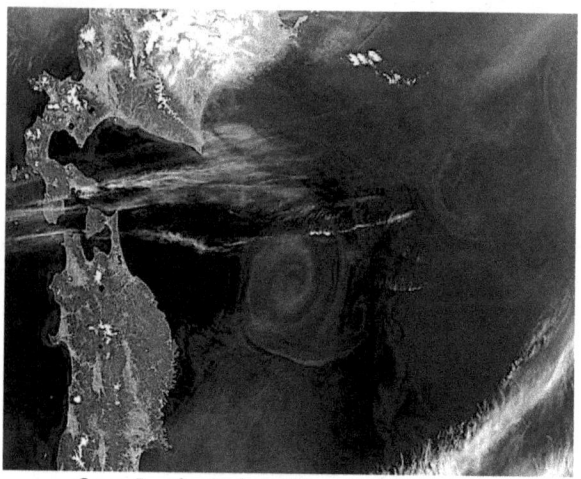

Great Pacific Garbage Heap (satellite image)

In terms of traffic jams and car crashes, we cannot rest with the representation of cars, lines of traffic and their concomitant desires. The petro-politics and use of products that derive from the extraction of oil has created a vast array of artificial life that should be included in this analysis of everyday life. Much of this life now makes its way into the ocean and becomes part of a vast array of objects that circulate in suspension. The North Pacific Gyre is a clockwise circulation of four prevailing ocean currents, and is in the process of collecting pelagic plastic, non-degradable chemical sludge, and other manmade debris in a huge oceanic suspension, convergent north of the Hawaiian archipelago. The Gyre concentrates an estimated 100 million tons of visible and invisible plastic waste, in what has been termed the "Great Pacific Garbage Patch." Various estimates on the size of the patch range from as large as Texas to the continental United States. Although, "most plastics break down slowly through a combination of photo-degradation, oxidation and mechanical abrasion . . . thick plastic items persist for decades, even when subject to direct sunlight, and survive even longer when shielded from UV radiation under water or in sediments" (Ryan et al. 2009, 1999). When the plastics do break down, the vast majority simply disassembles into ever finer microscopic fragments and, eventually, inassimilable molecular polymers. As such, the suspended, increasingly microscopic, waste builds up and is ingested by sea-life — birds, fish, zooplankton, plants, and other filter feeders. In recent studies, the microscopic suspension is measured to outweigh zooplankton by six times in relative mass (Ryan et al. 2000).

As such, the traffic jams and car crashes of human existence have translated into the seas. We are driving this process, and the global petro-political civilization does not relent from adding to this mass of plastics. Immanent materialism does not give us a solution to this picture of ecological Armageddon, yet it does enable an understanding of its formations. This understanding is penetrating; both in a rational sense of contemplating the scale of the problem, and in an unconscious sense of enabling creative work that can properly represent what is happening. One should appreciate the connection between everyday life and the most destructive production of pollution the world has ever known. The current situation requires radical and unheard of strategies and tactics to make the connection clear. I would like to suggest that the petro-citizen, immanent materialism, petro-politics, libidinal carism, and the international and time-based plateau into which the ideas of this letter fit, gives us a chance to communicate such a point.

§ Epilogue—Ode to Michael Douglas

In the film, *Falling Down* (1993), Michael Douglas gets out of his car in a traffic jam and fires a bazooka into a roadwork. His character represents a rebellion against the everyday conformity that traffic jams and car crashes can produce. We all feel this rebellion ebb and flow through us as we watch the spectacle on TV or are stuck in traffic jams. Yet the act of getting out of our cars and abandoning everyday life is anticipated for us through the regimes of economics in which we are now enmeshed. How will we pay off the mortgage or afford the rent if we don't go to work? What is the future of society if we stay in our homes, or only operate on foot? The wholesale non-use of cars or oil-driven public transport, or the switch to electric cars, is currently not possible, unless the means to work from home through networked jobs is more fully realised, and everything that we do is reorganised accordingly. Until that time in future history, we are consigned to the lives of commuters and the petro-citizenship that seeps into all we understand about social organization. Michael Douglas' character represents a type that should not be emulated; yet his drives exemplify the ways in which petro-citizenship is embedded in our behaviour. He turns to violence to sort out a traffic jam and deal with his frustrations at work in his domestic life. We should understand how this breaking point between petro-life and affect can be articulated through art and philosophy. Such articulation also constitutes survival narratives and escape routes from the plateau of the petro-citizen. For example, we should resist the depletion of planetary resources without reciprocity. This stopping point is a break from the past, and involves the integration of ecological mythology with pragmatic and sustainable ways to transform society and habit. I hope that immanent materialism could be part of this integration, as it recognises that art and creativity have a vital role to play in changing everyday life.

References

Ballard, J.G. 1973. *Crash*. London: Picador.

Barbrook, R. 2007. "The Holy Fools (Mute Mix)," *Imaginary Futures: From Thinking Machines to the Global Village* [group weblog]: http://www.imaginaryfutures.net/2007/04/14/the-holy-fools/.

Bennett, J. 2010. *Vibrant Matter: A Political Ecology of Things*. Durham: Duke University Press.

Brassier, Ray. 2011. "Concepts and Objects." In *The Speculative Turn: Continental Material-ism and Realism*, eds. Levi Bryant, Nick Srnicek, and Graham Harman, 47–66. Melbourne: re.press.

Cronenberg, D, dir. 1996. *Crash*. Toronto: Fine Line Features.

Coole, D. and S. Frost, eds. 2010. *New Materialisms: Ontology, Agency, and Politics*. Durham: Duke University Press.

de Certeau, M. 1988. *The Practice of Everyday Life*, trans. S. Rendall. Berkeley: University of California Press.

Deleuze, G. 1989. *Cinema II: The Time-Image*, trans. R. Galeta and H. Tomlinson. London: Continuum.

Deleuze, G. 1990. *The Logic of Sense*, trans. M. Lester and C. Stivale. New York: Columbia University Press.

Deleuze, G. 1995. *Negotiations*, trans. M. Joughin. New York: Columbia University Press.

Deleuze, G. 1997. *Essays Critical and Clinical*, trans. D.W. Smith and M.A. Greco. Minneapolis: University of Minnesota Press.

Deleuze, G. and F. Guattari. 1984. *Anti-Oedipus: Capitalism and Schizophrenia*, trans. R. Hurley, M. Seem & H.R. Lane. London: The Athlone Press.

Deleuze, G. and F. Guattari. 1988. *A Thousand Plateaus: Capitalism and Schizophrenia*, trans. B. Massumi. London: The Athlone Press

Focillon, Henri. 1992. *The Life of Forms in Art*. New York: Zone Books.

Gatens, M. 1996. "Through a Spinozist Lens: Ethology, Difference, Power." In *Deleuze: A Critical Reader*, ed. P. Patton, 162–187. Oxford: Blackwell.

Kant, I. 1933. *Immanuel Kant's Critique of Pure Reason*, trans. N.K. Smith. Basingstoke: Macmillan Education Ltd.

Kelly, K. 1999. *New Rules for the New Economy*. London: Fourth Estate.

Lefebvre, Henri. 2002. *The Critique of Everyday Life: Foundations for a Sociology of the Everyday*, Vol. 2, trans. J. Moore. London: Verso Books.

Negarestani, R. 2008. *Cyclonopedia: Complicity with Anonymous Materials*. Melbourne: re. press.

Nietzsche, F. 2001. *The Gay Science: With a Prelude in Rhymes*, trans. J. Naukhoff. Cambridge: Cambridge University Press.

Ryan, P.G. et al. 2009. "Monitoring the Abun-dance of Plastic Debris in the Marine Environment." *Philosophical Transactions of the Royal Society B* 364 (1526): 1999–2012.

Simondon, Gilbert. 1995. *L'individu et sa genèse physico-biologique*. Grenoble: Jerome Millon.

Toscano, A. 2010. "Petropolitics as Retro-politics: Oil and the Geopolitical Imagination." Paper presented at Goldsmiths College, University of London, Petropolitics Conference, October 2010: http://www.gold.ac.uk/media/Toscano_petropolitics_retropolitics.pdf.

Williams, J. 2009. "If Not Here, Then Where? On the Location and Individuation of Events in Badiou and Deleuze." *Deleuze Studies* 3: 97–123.

W. dreams, like Phaedrus, of an army of thinker-friends, thinker-lovers. He dreams of a thought-army, a thought-pack, which would storm the philosophical Houses of Parliament. He dreams of Tartars from the philosophical steppes, of thought-barbarians, thought-outsiders. What distances would shine in their eyes!

~Lars Iyer

www.babelworkinggroup.org

www.ingramcontent.com/pod-product-compliance
Lightning Source LLC
Chambersburg PA
CBHW070850160426
43192CB00012B/2380